795

AUG   1984

Exploring
the
Bayous

Exploring
the
Bayous

John L. Tveten

photographs by the author

David McKay Company, Inc.
New York

Acknowledgments

The author wishes to thank Carl H. Aiken III,
Associate Director of the Houston Museum
of Natural Science, and Ellen H. Goins for their
comments on the manuscript.

Library of Congress Cataloging in Publication Data

Tveten, John L
  Exploring the bayous.

  Includes index.
  SUMMARY: Explores life on the bayous, unique water-
ways found in the southern United States.
  1. Bayous—Juvenile literature. 2. Bayous—Southern
States—Juvenile literature. [1. Bayous] I. Title.
GB1203.8.T84   500.9′16′93   78-4418
ISBN 0-679-20601-9

1 2 3 4 5 6 7 8 9 10
Manufactured in the United States of America

To Gloria and Michael
*who have shared
the bayous with me*

Contents

1   A Day and Night on the Bayou   *1*
2   What Is a Bayou?   *5*
3   Plants of the Bayous   *9*
4   Animals of the Bayous   *23*
5   A Unique Environment   *49*
6   Louisiana: The Bayou State   *57*
7   Houston: City on a Bayou   *63*
8   Wealth from the Bayou   *69*
9   Hope for the Future   *79*
10   A Happy Ending   *81*
      Index   *85*

1

A Day and Night on the Bayou

THE WATERS OF the bayou are dark and mysterious—a slow moving stream that appears to have nowhere to go on a hot summer afternoon. A turtle suns itself on a lily pad. A great blue heron stands motionless on the bank. Everything is quiet.

But danger lurks beneath the water's surface. A long, dark shadow moves slowly and silently upstream. Fish dart for cover as it approaches, for the shadow is an alligator in search of food.

With scarcely a ripple, the 'gator rises to the surface. It looks very much like a floating log. The turtle dives quickly to the bottom to hide in the mud, while the heron takes wing with hoarse croaks of fright. There will be no dinner for the hungry alligator just now. But he is patient. Soon, he will catch a meal.

The alligator is king of the bayou.

The huge trees on the banks of the bayou are draped with gray-green curtains of Spanish moss. Small birds nest in the bushes. Butterflies dart about in the patches of sunlight. A pair of otters bound along the bank and slide headfirst down a mud slide into the bayou. Enjoying their game, they climb out and do it again.

As darkness falls, the night creatures take over. The frog chorus tunes up with a melody of croaks and trills. Great horned owls hoot in their deep bass voices; little screech owls call in their high-pitched ones. Barred owls repeat over and over, "Who cooks for you?"

Now the curtains of Spanish moss seem to hide the bayou's secrets. Bats dart out to catch flying insects. Tiny flying squirrels scamper in the branches and glide from tree to tree. A ring-tailed raccoon wanders out to search for clams, and a beaver swims along, pulling a freshly cut bush to its den beneath the bank.

The scream of a bobcat startles the other animals. With a loud smack of its flat tail on the surface, the beaver dives beneath the water. The raccoon looks quickly for shelter, and the scampering squirrels are suddenly still. For a time there is silence.

In the light of the moon, a pair of eyes can be seen on the surface of the water. The alligator is still on the prowl.

There are many creatures that make their homes in the water and on the banks of the bayou. Some come out by day; others prowl at night. Some are hunters; others are hunted. Life here is always an adventure.

2

What Is a Bayou?

THE WORD BAYOU, pronounced by-oo, is the Louisiana French version of the early Choctaw Indian word, *bayuk,* meaning a small stream. Geographers use the name for a watercourse that is the outlet of a river or lake. However, most people in the bayou country of the South call almost any kind of stream or small river a bayou.

Louisiana is usually considered the bayou state because thousands of small bayous crisscross the land. It would be almost impossible to count them all, and many have no names. There are also bayous in other southern states, such as Texas, Arkansas, Mississippi, and Alabama.

In eastern Texas, where a number of French people once settled, many of the streams are still called bayous. Farther south, along the Texas coast near

Some bayous flow quietly through the forest, while others wander across open marshes lined with houses built on stilts.

A bayou is sometimes an oasis of green in the midst of subdivisions and industrial plants.

Mexico, the same kinds of streams are called rivers or creeks.

Bayous are usually slow, sluggish, winding waterways. Some are small enough to step across. Others are as wide and deep as large rivers. They form a spiderweb of watery threads across the land. Some seem to go nowhere. Others are avenues to the sea.

Because they flow through different kinds of countryside, not all bayous look alike. Some twist and wander through dense forests of towering trees or flow through vast open marshes of reeds and long grasses. Others that begin inland and reach to the coast run through all these different habitats.

3

Plants of the Bayous

PLANTS THAT GROW together in particular places are called plant communities or plant associations. There are many such communities along the bayous.

On higher ground, where it is not too wet, are many kinds of hardwood, or broadleaf, trees. Most are deciduous; that is, they lose their leaves in winter. In the hardwood forests are oaks of many different kinds—red and white oaks, water oaks, willow and laurel oaks, and a species whose acorn cups are so large it is called the basket oak. Here, too, are elms, ironwoods, beeches, hackberries, hollies, maples, dogwoods, and redbuds.

One interesting tree, typical of the bayous, is the southern magnolia. Its dark green leaves are nearly a foot long, and its white flowers are the size of dinner plates. Although it is a broad-leaved tree, it is also an evergreen—a plant that keeps its leaves throughout the winter.

The flowers of the southern magnolia are the size of dinner plates.

Beneath the trees of the hardwood forest are dozens of kinds of shrubs and vines. Wild flowers bloom throughout much of the year, for it seldom gets very cold in the bayou country.

Pine forests are also found along the bayous. These evergreen trees, with needlelike leaves, reproduce by means of cones. There are pine trees all across the continent, but the species of the bayous are best adapted to the moist, warm climate of the South and Southeast. The major species are the loblolly, slash, shortleaf, and longleaf pines.

Trees are important to the animals that live along the bayou. Some creatures prefer the forests of hardwoods, while others like the pines. Birds nest in the branches and search for insects which feed on the leaves. Both birds and mammals eat the fruit of the trees—berries, acorns, pine cones, and other seeds. Tree frogs cling to the trunks, and insects burrow beneath the bark. Each tree is a small zoo, filled with creatures large and small.

Most fascinating of all the bayou plant communities are the great cypress swamps of the lowlands, where the bayous overflow and spill their waters across the land. These swamps are the bayou's wildest areas— places where few people come and where many rare animals find refuge from civilization.

The cypress and tupelo trees of the swamp are especially adapted to live in the water. Their trunks are very broad and swollen at the base to help them stand in the soft mud. The cypress also puts up strange growths, or "knees," from its roots. These stick up above the water and may help carry air to the sub-

A green treefrog uses its suction-cup toes to cling to a tree branch draped with Spanish moss.

Opposite:
Cypress knees stick up above the surface of the swamp.

merged roots. Although the cypress has needlelike leaves and cones and is related to the pines, it is not evergreen. Instead, it loses its needles and is bare during the winter. Hence, its full name: bald cypress.

Near the Gulf Coast, the land becomes even flatter and lower. Here there are vast marshlands, where only grasses, reeds, and water plants grow. Because the water stands throughout the year, the soil is too wet for trees.

The bayous here wind through seas of grass. Early settlers in Louisiana called this "the trembling prairie," because it seems to be half land, half water. In this open country there is more sunlight, and the wild flowers are bigger and brighter than elsewhere. In spring, the entire marsh is carpeted with all the colors of the rainbow. Water lilies grow in the bayous, sending up their platter-size, round leaves to float on the surface.

Some of the bayous in both the marshes and the swamps are filled with floating water hyacinths. Their bright green leaves and orchidlike flowers make them one of the most beautiful of all the plants. But they are also a terrible nuisance because they grow so fast and so thickly that they fill the bayous and sometimes prevent boats from getting through them.

There are both freshwater and saltwater marshes. Where the bayous flow into the Gulf of Mexico or its bays, tides push salt water upstream. Different kinds of plants grow in fresh and salt water. And different kinds of animals live there as well.

Water which has some salt, but not as much as the

14

Both the flowers and the large, round leaves of the white water lily float on the surface so the plant can be pollinated and get sunlight to manufacture food.

sea, is called brackish. Brackish-water marshes occur between the fresh and salt zones. The amount of salt depends on how much fresh water is flowing down the bayou and how much salt water is being pushed up by tidal and wind action. The brackish marsh, too, has its own plants and animals. As a bayou nears the Gulf, the water changes from fresh to brackish to salt water. Each zone is important, for each provides a home for species unable to live elsewhere.

Not all the coastal land is flat. Out of the marsh-lands rise occasional small, round hills. These are often salt domes, made by earth that is pushed up by deposits of salt below. Because it is drier on the hills, live oaks and other trees can grow. These groves are called oak mottes.

Also along the shores of the Gulf are low ridges of sand, mud, and shell. They have been formed by powerful hurricane winds and waves that pile debris above the beach. Here, too, trees can grow, and their roots help trap more soil and keep the ridges from being washed away. These ridges are called cheniers, after the French word, *chêne,* which means oak. As you might expect, live oaks thrive on the cheniers.

The live oak is evergreen. Old leaves fall only as they are replaced by new ones, and the trees stay green throughout the year. Their trunks grow up to several feet thick, and they have spreading, twisted branches. In the branches grows another plant typical of the South: Spanish moss. It thrives not only on the live oaks but in the swamps as well. In spite of its name, it is not a moss, but a flowering plant of the *bromeliad,* or air plant, family. Many of its relatives are popular

Spanish moss is not really a moss. It is a bromeliad with tiny yellow-green flowers.

house plants. The cultivated pineapple is also a bromeliad.

Spanish moss is not a parasite of trees. It makes its own food with the help of *chlorophyll,* the green coloring matter in its slender leaves and stems, and does not harm its host. Except for the fact that it needs the shade and moisture provided by trees, it could grow just as well on wires or posts.

Throughout the forests and swamps along the bayous are bogs—low, damp places with acidic soil, where sphagnum moss, wild orchids, and several kinds of ferns grow. Bogs are very special places because they contain many rare and interesting plant species.

In the bogs there are also plants that eat insects. Called carnivorous, or meat-eating, plants, they trap tiny creatures and digest them, thereby getting nitrogen to help them grow. These plants have several different methods of catching their food. Pitcher-plants have vase-shaped leaves that hold water and plant juices. Inside, the surface is waxy and covered with

Opposite:
Four types of carnivorous plants are found in the bayou country: (1) The yellow pitcher plant captures insects in its vase-shaped leaves. (2) Above the water, the floating bladderwort has pretty yellow blossoms; below the water, its threadlike leaves are covered with little chambers that trap minute water creatures. (3) The sticky leaves of the sundew trap careless insects. (4) Below its pink flowers, the dwarf butterwort has a rosette of sticky, flypaper leaves.

1

2

3

4

downward-pointing hairs. Insects, crawling on a leaf, fall in and cannot get out. They are then digested by the juices.

Other carnivorous plants include sundews and butterworts, with sticky leaves that catch their prey like flypaper. The leaves curl around the victims and absorb them.

Bladderworts have still another kind of trap. Beneath the surface of the water, these floating plants have tiny hollow chambers, or bladders. When little water creatures brush against the chambers, a trapdoor flies open and they are sucked in. The door shuts again and the bladderwort has another meal.

From the giant spreading live oak to the tiny sundew, there are thousands of different plants that grow in and along the bayous. Some are familiar to everyone; others are seldom seen. Each, however, is important, for it plays its own part in the balance of nature. No matter how small or rare a plant might be, there may be other creatures that depend on it for food or shelter.

4

Animals of the Bayous

JUST AS THERE are many plants along the bayous, there are also many animals. They range in size from microscopic organisms to large snakes, fish, birds, and mammals. Some live in the water; others live in the surrounding forests, swamps, or marshes. But all are dependent on the water for survival.

King of the bayou fishes is the alligator gar. With its long, beaklike snout filled with sharp teeth, it looks like something from the age of dinosaurs. And this, in fact, is what it is, for the gar is a very primitive fish that has changed little in millions of years. Its scales are hard and thick, and it grows to an enormous size. Many weigh more than 100 pounds, and some may reach 300.

There are also tiny minnows, which serve as food for larger fish and for many other animals. Some of the small fish are young and will grow larger if they survive. But others will get no bigger. Many kinds of minnows remain small even as adults.

Fishermen come to the bayous to catch largemouth bass, crappies, and several kinds of sunfish, often called bream or perch. There are also freshwater drum with the strange name of gaspergou and large catfish. All of these make the freshwater bayous popular fishing places for people as well as for wildlife.

In the salt water and brackish parts of the bayous are other fish from the bays and Gulf of Mexico. They swim into the shallow water to lay their eggs, and the young find shelter among the marsh grasses. Here are high-jumping mullet and croakers, which make grunting sounds when handled. Here, too, are flounder, redfish, and many other species.

Fish are not the only residents of the bayou waters, however. Clams and snails burrow along the bottom or cling to water plants. Crabs and shrimp swim upstream from the bays, and their freshwater cousins, the crayfish, live in almost every pond and puddle.

Some mammals, such as beavers, are largely aquatic and spend most of their time in the bayou. Beavers are not as abundant as they were in the early days of the fur traders, but they are now becoming more common again.

In the South, however, beavers seldom build large dams or stick houses. Instead they burrow into the banks of the bayous and live inside the tunnels. They come out to feed mainly at night, and are seldom seen by people. Their presence is indicated by trees and bushes which have been cut down or stripped of bark.

Crayfish are found in nearly every pond, puddle, and stream. They are eaten by many other animals, as well as by people.

The playful otters of the bayous are excellent swimmers—as much at home in the water as on land. They feed on fish, frogs, crayfish, and other aquatic animals. Their close relative, the mink, also catches part of its food in bayou waters.

Muskrats build their dome-shaped houses throughout the marshes, and their territory is now shared by the larger nutria, which was introduced to the Gulf Coast from South America. These large water rats eat vegetation, and they make themselves unpopular by feeding in rice and sugarcane fields.

Beavers, muskrats, and nutria are the largest and most aquatic of the rodents, but there are many others that live in the woods, fields, and marshes of the bayou country. Best known are the gray and fox squirrels that scamper about in the trees during the daytime and the shy and beautiful flying squirrels that come out at night.

Flying squirrels don't really fly, but they can glide for long distances by stretching out the membranes between their front and hind legs.

A dozen different kinds of mice and rats live along the bayous. Most are harmless native species, seldom seen by people. Other mammals that are seldom seen include shrews (the smallest mammals of all), moles, and pocket gophers. All stay hidden underground or in fallen logs or crevices during the daytime. Bats also come out at dusk to feed on flying insects. They are sometimes seen in the air over the bayous or around lights, but it is difficult to tell one kind of bat from another in flight. Actually, there are a dozen species which help to control the insect populations.

Otters feed on fish and other water creatures.

Raccoons, bobcats, skunks, red and gray foxes, and coyotes are other residents of bayou-land. Although some of them live by catching and killing other animals, none is a threat to humans. The predatory bobcat is no more dangerous to people who leave him alone than the cute little cottontail or the swamp rabbit.

White-tailed deer are found nearly everywhere, and scientists have found an interesting race of white-tails in the Louisiana marshes. They have larger hooves than other deer, so they don't sink as deeply into the mud.

Two of the most famous and interesting animals of the South are the opossum and the armadillo. The opossum (called a possum) looks very much like a giant rat, with its long snout and naked tail. But it is the bayou's only member of the group of mammals called marsupials—animals that have pouches in which they raise their young. When baby opossums are born, they are less than half an inch long. Several of them could fit in a teaspoon. Blind and helpless, they climb into the mother's pouch, where they nurse and stay for more than two months. When they finally are large enough to come out, they often ride around on their mother's back, holding on with their tails. When frightened, opossums may roll over, close their eyes, and appear dead. From this behavior we get the expression "playing possum."

The armadillo, with its peculiar shell, looks very much like a little tank. In fact, the name comes from the Spanish and means "little armored one." With

Opposite:
Flying squirrels are beautiful little animals that
sail from tree to tree.

The opossum uses its long tail to help it climb through the trees and vines.

Opposite:
White-tailed deer are common throughout the bayou country. This doe is well camouflaged in the long grass, but she can run very fast if danger threatens.

An armadillo emerges from its hole.

their long claws, armadillos are exceptional diggers. They live in burrows, and their diet is mainly insects. A century ago, there were no armadillos in the area. But they evidently crossed the Rio Grande from Mexico into Texas, and gradually wandered northward. Now they are common throughout eastern Texas and Louisiana.

More than 300 species of birds can be found in the bayou country. Some are permanent residents, while others nest there in summer but go south in winter to the tropical climates of Central or South America. Still others come to the bayous' woods and marshes for the winter after nesting in the northern states or in Canada. Many birds only pause during their long migratory flights. They can be seen in the spring or fall as they stop to rest or feed on journeys that cover thousands of miles. Returning north in spring, they fly nonstop across the Gulf of Mexico. If the weather is good, they have little trouble. But if they must fly in rain or strong winds, they have to stop and rest as soon as they reach the Texas or Louisiana coast. At these times, the trees of the oak mottes and cheniers are filled with tired birds. This spring migration is a spectacular thing to see. There may be thousands of thrushes, orioles, and vireos. Blue- and rose-breasted grosbeaks, scarlet tanagers, indigo and painted buntings, and nearly thirty kinds of warblers look like miniature rainbows in the live oak trees. Bird-watchers come from all over the United States and from other countries to see the birds when they return to the bayous.

In winter, other species flock to these southern

33

The yellow-breasted chat (top) and the scarlet tanager (bottom) are only two of the brilliantly colored birds that migrate through the bayou country.

states. Huge clouds of ducks and geese make the marshes their winter home. When ice and snow cover most of the country, they seek refuge where the water seldom freezes and they can always find food.

Blackbirds come by the millions to the marshes, and gulls and terns spend the winter along the shore. Sandpipers of many kinds can be seen in the bays and marshes, too. When warm weather returns, these birds head northward again. But others remain through the hot summer to lay their eggs and raise their young.

When most of the ducks and geese are gone, the tall, long-legged herons remain in the grassy marshes. They spear fish in the shallow water and nest together in large colonies in patches of low bushes and reeds. Fifteen different species of herons are found here.

Farther upstream along the bayous, other birds nest in the trees of the forests. Mockingbirds and Carolina wrens sing to tell others that this is their territory. Brilliant red cardinals, sleek wood thrushes, and noisy but beautiful blue jays all settle down to raise families.

In the deep swamp, among the moss-covered cypress trees and the thickets of willow and button-bush, live still other species. Here the red-shouldered hawk and the barred owl hunt for rodents and other small animals. The hawk hunts by day; the owl by night.

Long-necked anhingas swim slowly along, looking for fish to spear with their sharp dagger-like beaks. Also called water turkeys or snakebirds, they some-times swim submerged with just their necks out of

A young anhinga perches on a dead tree near the water.

Opposite:

The great egret is one of the members of the heron family that nests and feeds along the bayou. Its long legs enable it to wade through the water, and its sharp beak is an effective fish spear.

water. Then, perched on a dead tree, they spread out their wings to dry.

Loud drumming sounds are made by pileated woodpeckers, digging into tree trunks in search of insects. As large as crows, they are black, with white wing patches and flaming red crests on their heads. They nest in holes they drill in trees, and the holes are often used by other birds as well. A large pileated woodpecker hole might house a colorful wood duck the next year. Other woodpecker holes are used by screech owls, chickadees, titmice, bluebirds, and yellow prothonotary warblers. This is a good example of how one wild creature may depend on another.

No creature is more typical of the bayou country than the alligator. Largest of all our reptiles, it has no enemies as an adult except human beings. A big 'gator can reach sixteen feet in length. In fact, the record is more than nineteen feet.

Alligators live in almost all the large swamps, bayous, and marshes along the Gulf Coast. They are often seen sunning themselves on the banks, or floating in the water with just their nostrils and eyes above the surface. The loud bellowing roar of the bulls can be a scary sound in the dark bayou.

The female builds a nest mound of grasses and other plants beside the water. She buries her eggs in the nest, and then stays nearby to guard them. This is unusual for a reptile, for most of them abandon their eggs as soon as they are laid.

Baby alligators are only about nine inches long when they hatch. They are black with yellow bands, but as they grow, they lose their markings. Many large

Baby alligators are only a few inches long when they hatch from their eggs.

birds, mammals, turtles, fish, and even other alligators prey on the babies, but enough survive to continue the cycle.

It is people who are the major threat to the alligator because they use the skins for shoes and purses. (A single alligator hide is worth a great deal of money.) Because alligators were becoming rare in recent years, they were put on the government's endangered-species list and protected. Some people in the swamps still poach, or hunt them illegally, but alligators are becoming more common again.

Snakes are probably the most feared of all the bayou creatures, yet there are many more harmless than poisonous ones. In fact, snakes are very important to the environment because they help to control the rat and mouse populations.

Certainly, a few species should be left alone. The poisonous cottonmouth, or "water moccasin," can be found around almost any body of water. A dangerous snake, it normally grows to three or four feet in length. Cottonmouths stand their ground when disturbed and strike readily.

Three other major types of poisonous snakes are also found throughout the bayou country. Copperheads live in both the upland forests and the swamps, and they are well camouflaged among the fallen leaves. The very pretty, but venomous, coral snake, as well as rattlesnakes that range in size from the large canebrake to the little pygmy, are also found here. But in spite of the number of poisonous snakes, very few people are bitten. More people die each year

The venomous cottonmouth stands its ground when cornered.

This little broad-banded water snake may grow quite large, but it is completely harmless.

from allergic reactions to wasp stings than from the bites of poisonous snakes.

Even most of the water snakes found along the bayous are relatively harmless. They might bite if handled, but they are not poisonous. Racers, rat snakes, king snakes, and striped garter and ribbon snakes are all common and beneficial to the environment.

It is interesting to see how the different snakes protect themselves. While they are hunting for food, larger creatures are also hunting for them. The tiny brown earth snake burrows into dirt and among fallen leaves, where it is well camouflaged. The slender green snake pursues insects and small frogs through the leaves of the bushes and trees. Its long, thin body helps it to climb, and its color makes it hard to see. When cornered, the hognose snake flattens its neck and hisses. It tries to look as dangerous as possible. If that doesn't work, it rolls over on its back and plays dead. Each has its own means of protection and equipment for survival.

Sharing the forests and swamps with the snakes are several different kinds of lizards. A favorite of most people is the green anole, or "chameleon." Although it is not a true chameleon, it can change its color from green to brown.

Most unusual, perhaps, is the glass lizard, or "glass snake." Although it is a true lizard, it has no legs. With its long, slender body, it does look more like a snake. However, it is stiffer than a snake, and has ear openings and eyelids which snakes don't have. When grabbed by the tail, the glass lizard simply breaks it off and escapes. That is how it got its name. It then grows a new tail.

Box turtles crawl through the bayou woods, feeding on green plants, berries, mushrooms, and insects. And an assortment of water turtles—mud turtles, map turtles, painted turtles, sliders, and soft-shelled turtles—can often be seen sunning themselves on floating logs or along the banks.

Largest of the turtles are the common and alligator snappers. The latter gets its name from its huge head and sharp jaws. It lies on the bottom of the bayou with its mouth open and wiggles a little flap of skin that looks like a pink worm. When fish come to eat it, they are eaten instead. Alligator snapping turtles often weigh more than one hundred pounds.

Along with the reptiles, there are many amphibians who make their homes in the bayous: salamanders that look somewhat like lizards, but are slow moving and have wet, slimy skin; and toads that live on dry land and return to the water to lay their eggs.

Frogs come in all sizes—from the large bullfrog to the tiny cricket frog. Some species live mainly in the water, while others, such as the little tree frogs and chorus frogs, prefer to sit in the bushes and trees. Frogs are the favorite food of many other animals of the bayou.

Least popular of the bayou insects are probably the mosquitoes and biting flies. They often swarm through the swamps and marshes, making life unpleasant not only for people but for the animals that live there as well. But they are important, for they provide food for birds, bats, fish, and even other insects.

Opposite
*Shiny silver spots decorate the underwings of a
gulf fritillary butterfly*

*The deep-voiced "chug-a-rum" of the bullfrog
is a familiar sound along the bayou.*

The huge eyes of a watchful dragonfly are alert for passing insects.

The most beautiful insects are the butterflies. And because of the warm climate, the bayous have many large and colorful ones. The biggest are the swallowtails, named for the long tails on their hind wings. There are several different kinds that are as large as a person's hand.

Beetles, too, abound. Some tunnel into trees, while others crawl along the ground or through the leaves and grasses. Some even live in the water.

The unseen insects are those that live beneath the surface of the bayou. Many flying insects have young or larval stages which live in the water. Almost everyone recognizes the adult dragonfly. But few realize that young dragonflies are aquatic, and live in the bayous, where they catch tiny water creatures. Adults are sometimes called "mosquito hawks" because they catch mosquitoes on the wing. Young dragonflies eat mosquito larvae in the water.

5

A Unique Environment

THE WEATHER OF the bayou country helps to make it a
unique environment. Summers are generally hot, and
the warm weather lasts well into late autumn. Even in
midwinter, the temperature does not stay below freez-
ing for very long. There is seldom snow or ice. The
rainfall averages more than fifty inches each year, and
the humidity is very high. This means that there is
usually plenty of water in the bayous and marshes.
Warm temperatures and a constant supply of water
assure plenty of food for wildlife. Generally, the
warmer and wetter an area is, the more species of
plants and animals it can support.

The flocks of thousands and thousands of geese,
ducks, and shorebirds depend upon finding this safe
refuge when they head south. If something were to
destroy part of this winter habitat, it would have a
serious effect on bird populations. Even more critical,

Two baby great horned owls peer from their nest in a hollow tree.

however, is the role of the bayous as breeding grounds for both land and water creatures. In addition to the many birds, mammals—both large and small—raise their families where they have food, water, and shelter.

The marshes and the bays, where the bayous meet the Gulf of Mexico, are tremendously important for fish and shellfish. They spawn, or lay their eggs, in the warm shallow water, where they hide among the reeds and grass. Here, the young find shelter until they are large enough to protect themselves. Without this critical habitat, we would have fewer tasty fish, crabs, and shrimp to eat.

Ecology is defined in Webster's dictionary as simply "the branch of biology that deals with the relationships between living organisms and their sur- roundings." In other words, ecologists study how plants and animals get along together.

The simplest relationships to understand are those involving food. All living things need food of one kind or another. Most creatures are both the hunters and the hunted. Only green plants can make their own food. They are eaten by animals, and the animals, in turn, are eaten by other animals. These sequences are called food chains. Every living thing is involved in many such chains. For example, a delicate flower makes its food with the energy of the sun. It is then eaten by a caterpillar, which is later eaten by a dragonfly. Next the dragonfly is caught in a spider's web. A lizard then eats the spider, and a snake eats the lizard. Finally a hungry hawk feeds on the snake. So, in a way, the hawk is dependent on the flower for its dinner. All the plants and animals of the bayou are

51

A green anole lizard eats a caterpillar and becomes the next link in a food chain. Later, another animal may catch the anole.

important. If something happens to one, it affects the others. It also affects us.

Some of the plants and animals that once lived along the bayous are gone; others are becoming very rare. When the early settlers arrived, the forests teemed with black bears. Even President Theodore Roosevelt came to the Louisiana bayou country to hunt them. "Bears were plentiful," he wrote in his journal in 1907. Now bears are almost gone from Louisiana. The same is true of the red wolf and the cougar, or panther. Passenger pigeons that came by the thousands are extinct. And the Louisiana flock of tall whooping cranes has disappeared. Somewhere in the swamps, a huge ivory-billed woodpecker might still remain, but that species may also be extinct.

Some of these animals were killed by hunters, but hunting is now controlled with proper seasons and limits. A greater threat to the bayous is civilization, its farms and factories. Poisons have also taken their toll. In the 1940s, DDT was developed. The chemical worked well as an insecticide, but it killed other things as well. Washed into the bayous, it affected birds that ate the fish. Their eggs had thin shells that broke easily, or did not hatch. The osprey, or fish hawk, and the bald eagle have been victims of DDT. So has the brown pelican, the state bird of Louisiana. With new laws banning the use of some insecticides, these birds are coming back. But the recovery is very slow.

No one knows how many bayou plants may also be endangered. Trees, shrubs, and wild flowers are disappearing as new highways are built and swamps are drained. In some places, Spanish moss is being killed by air pollution. Botanists are now discovering which plants are in trouble, and are seeking ways to save them. If they are lost, they can never be replaced.

The wildlife picture is not entirely a dark one. There are success stories, too. One such story is the return of the egrets—tall, white members of the heron family that live in the swamps and marshes throughout the bayous. In the nineteenth century, it was stylish for ladies to wear egret and other feathers on their hats. The long white plumes of the egret were worth as much as a dollar apiece, and they were shipped to milliners by the train-carload. By 1900, egrets had almost vanished from the South.

When Edward McIlhenny found eight small egrets in a swamp, he brought them to his home on Avery Island in the Louisiana marsh country. He raised and released them, but the next year they returned there to nest. Soon, there were hundreds, then thousands of egrets. The colony remains on Avery Island today, and many people come to see them, as well as the beautiful gardens. The work by McIlhenny and new laws to protect birds brought the big white egrets back to the bayous, and now they are common.

Plants and animals have also been brought to the bayous from other countries. These are called introduced species. But these species often cause problems, for their natural enemies no longer keep them under control.

One example of this is the water hyacinth, a South American plant brought to the International Cotton Exposition in New Orleans, Louisiana, in 1884 The beautiful flowers were given away as souvenirs, and soon the city's fountains and pools and the surrounding bayous were filled with water hyacinths. In spite of their beauty, the plants present a problem because they often choke the waterways. Besides having seeds, they also produce new little plants from their roots. They can double in number in two weeks, and one plant can become thousands in a single season. They have been pulled up, mowed, and poisoned in efforts to open the streams—but with little success. The government spends millions of dollars each year in its attempt to control the population of water hyacinths and other introduced plants.

The nutria, or coypu, also came to the bayous from South America. Several of these big three-foot-long water rats were brought to Avery Island in 1938 and kept in a pen. Like most rodents, they reproduced rapidly. Later, in 1938, a hurricane damaged the pen and some of the animals escaped. Within five years, they had spread throughout southern Louisiana. Today, the nutria is the most important fur-bearing animal in the state. Their furs are worth nearly seven million dollars, and more than a million are trapped each year.

There is another side to the nutria story, however. It was hoped that the animal would help to control water hyacinths and other troublesome weeds. But it seems to prefer eating rice and sugarcane from farmers' fields.

Starlings were brought to New York from Europe about 1900, by a man who wanted America to have all the birds mentioned in the plays of Shakespeare. Now starlings are abundant everywhere. They eat grain from the fields and take away nests from our native birds, and they are partly responsible for the decline of bluebirds and other species which also nest in holes in trees.

These are only three examples of introduced species which have made themselves at home in the bayou country. There are many others, such as the corbicula, or Asian clam, which is spreading throughout the waterways. Although the clam is a favorite food of raccoons, it may crowd out other species and become a nuisance.

6

Louisiana: The Bayou State

THE HEART OF the bayou country is in Louisiana. Here, the Mississippi River wanders for 600 miles through the state to empty finally into the Gulf of Mexico. At the mouth of the river, where it flows into the Gulf, it has built a large delta—new land made from mud and sand carried down by the river.

When the river is flowing rapidly, it carries large amounts of silt. When it reaches the ocean, it slows down, and the silt drops to the bottom. As the silt builds up, new land is formed. During thousands of years, the Mississippi has changed its course several times and has built several deltas. Through the low, flat delta region are many little bayous. In fact, nearly half the state of Louisiana is below the high-water level of the Mississippi and other large rivers. When floods occur, new bayous are sometimes formed, and old ones disappear.

Native American tribes, such as the Attakapa (pronounced Tackapaw) and the Chitimacha first lived along the bayous. Then the Spanish explorers came, and they were followed by the early settlers, many of whom were French. In fact, most of the larger bayous still have either Indian or French names—Teche, Plaquemine, Bouef, Lafourche, for example.

Among these early settlers were the Acadians, French people who had helped to colonize Acadia (now called Nova Scotia) in eastern Canada. During the war between England and France, Acadia was captured by the British, and the Acadians were deported in 1755.

Because the British were afraid the Acadians would join with other French people in Canada and cause trouble, they burned their homes and separated the families. Some of the American colonies would not take them in, and the Acadians wandered about, seeking a place to live. When some of them heard there were French people in Louisiana, they came to New Orleans. But rather than live in the busy city, they moved up the bayous into the wilderness. Word spread, and other Acadians came. Soon, there was a large colony along the bayous. They built their homes from cypress trees and made their living from the land.

Over the years, the name was shortened from Acadian to Cadien, and then to Cajun. Southern Louisiana is still called Cajun country today, and descendants of the original Acadians still remain.

The Cajuns are a warm, friendly people, with a language of their own. Cajun music and Cajun cooking are famous throughout the country.

A typical Acadian house along the bayou had an outside stairway. This house is now in the Acadian Village near Lafayette, Louisiana.

One of the most famous legends about the Acadians is Longfellow's poem, "Evangeline," which describes how a young couple were separated upon deportation from Canada and how they searched for each other across the country. Some say the story is a true one; others claim it is not. But whether fact or fiction, the area around the town of St. Martinville and the Bayou Teche is still known as "Evangeline country."

Following the French to the bayous were the Anglos—English and "Yankees" from the East. This new era in the bayou country was a time of cotton and sugarcane plantations, of art, music, and fancy parties, and a time of steamboats on the bayou.

The Bayou Teche is one of the most beautiful of all Louisiana's bayous. An ancient path of the Mississippi River, it winds through more than 150 miles of rich, fertile land. Indian legend says that when a huge silver snake terrorized the region, Indian warriors killed the snake with arrows and clubs. As it was dying in agony, its twisting body cut grooves in the earth. These later filled with water and formed the bayou. It was originally called *Tenche,* the Native American word for snake, but this was later changed to Teche.

Along the Teche are great stands of live oak trees, which once shaded huge plantation mansions—magnificent homes, with white columns and furniture imported from Europe.

Fortunes were made from these plantations, and fortunes were spent. For example, one plantation owner imported thousands of spiders to provide decorations for his daughters' wedding. He had his servants place the spiders in the trees along the entrance lane. When the spiders had covered the trees with webs, the webs were dusted with powdered silver and gold.

This was the time of the romantic South. Richard Taylor, a Louisiana Confederate officer, wrote about the Teche before the Civil War: "In all my wanderings, and they have been many and wide, I cannot recall so fair, so bountiful, and so happy a land."

Today, some of the old homes still stand with their ghosts of the past, and many can be visited.

Life in the bayou country is changing, however. The discovery of oil in Louisiana has brought in new industry, new towns, and new people. Now there are helicopters to take oilmen to their jobs. But there are still reminders of the old way of life. Some people still carry on the traditions of their Acadian ancestors. And hunting and fishing still provide a living for the people of the swamp.

The largest wild swamp left in the United States is the Atchafalaya, a Choctaw Indian word meaning "long river." The swamp lies between the natural levees, or high banks, of the Mississippi River and the levees of the Bayou Teche. A giant basin only a foot or two above sea level, it covers more than a million acres.

Through the basin runs the Atchafalaya River that helps carry off water from the Mississippi system. Each spring, when snow and ice melt farther north, the Atchafalaya becomes a raging flood and fills the basin with water.

Because there are no roads through the center of the swamp, transportation is by boat, through hundreds of winding bayous and channels. Although the swamp is still the home of deer, cottonmouths, eagles, and alligators, the boats have changed with the times. The early swamp people used the pirogue—the Louisiana version of the canoe. It was made from a single hollowed-out cypress log and pushed with a pole. It could, the locals said, "ride on a heavy dew." There are still pirogues in the swamp, but now they are made of plywood. And they might be pushed by outboard motors.

Fishing is big business in the Atchafalaya. Sport fishermen come to fish for bass, crappie, bream, and catfish. Commercial fishermen catch many species with nets, lines, and traps set throughout the swamp. They also take crabs, crayfish, bullfrogs, and turtles. These, as well as the fish, bring high prices at restaurants and stores in the cities.

Deer, squirrels, raccoons, opossums, ducks, and geese are hunted in the Atchafalaya. Besides shooting game for food, the local people may serve as guides for other hunters.

One of the most unusual occupations in the swamp is "gathering moss." Spanish moss is pulled from the trees with long hooks and cured, or treated, to remove the green covering. The inside fibers resemble horsehair. In early Louisiana, the moss was used for many purposes. It was mixed with mud to make bricks, or to fill cracks in houses. It was also spun and braided to make bridles, and it was woven into saddle blankets and horse collars. A great deal of it was sold commercially for upholstering furniture and mattresses. Today, man-made fibers have replaced Spanish moss, but there are still a few "moss pickers" in the swamp.

7

Houston: City on a Bayou

BAYOUS ARE ALSO found in eastern Texas. They flow through the remaining forests of the Big Thicket—once a heavily wooded wilderness—and across the coastal prairies before they drain into the bays along the Texas coast.

Houston is the fifth largest city in the United States. Located about thirty miles inland, it was built on a bayou to provide transportation to the Gulf of Mexico. It is now a space center and oil capital, but without the bayou it might never have existed. Houston still calls itself the Bayou City.

Native Americans originally camped along the bayous near what is now Houston. They hunted and fished and gathered oysters and clams from the bays. Signs of their camps can still be found in many places on the bayou banks, and archaeologists are learning about Native American culture by examining the

63

artifacts in these sites. In the old midden heaps, or garbage dumps, they find shells, bones, pieces of pottery, stone arrowheads, and tools.

French and Spanish missionaries came to these bayous in the first half of the eighteenth century, but most of the missions did not last long because the mosquito-infested marshes, disease, and unfriendly Indians drove them away.

Finally, about 1820, a few people began to settle in the coastal plain near Houston, where they cut timber and grew crops. They, too, depended on the bayous for transportation and for food.

Even the notorious pirate, Jean Lafitte, came to this part of the Texas coast in the early 1800s. He and his crew made their headquarters on Barataria Bay in the Mississippi delta of Louisiana. From this fortress, they sailed out to raid ships and capture goods all along the Gulf. Lafitte set up other bases along the coast and moved up and down the twisting bayous. In this maze of waterways it was almost impossible to find and capture him.

In 1832, Augustus C. Allen and John K. Allen arrived in Texas from New York. They invested their money in land and did very well. Then they bought the land at the head of a stream called Buffalo Bayou for about one dollar an acre. Here they founded a new town and named it Houston in honor of their friend, General Sam Houston, the hero of the battle for Texas's independence from Mexico and a leading candidate for president of the new Republic of Texas. The Allen brothers hoped their town would soon become the capital city of the Republic.

On August 30, 1836, the Allens placed an advertisement in a newspaper, in which they offered lots for sale in Houston. Among other things, the long advertisement said:

"The town of Houston is located at a point on the river which must ever command the trade of the largest and richest portion of Texas."

The Allen brothers were right. It was a good site for a town. The pioneers needed supplies, and the cheapest way of transporting them was by water. Most Texas streams flooded in spring and ran dry in summer. And they had sandbars and logjams which caused problems for boats.

But Buffalo Bayou was fairly deep, wide, and clear. It did not run dry, and it flowed into Galveston Bay, one of the best harbors on the Texas coast. The head of the bayou was near fertile farming land, and there was plenty of timber for building and pure drinking water.

Three months after the Allens' advertisement, Houston was chosen as the capital of the Republic of Texas. (It remained the capital city until 1839.) Within a year, Houston's population grew to 1,500 people. Soon, it was a center for agriculture, textile factories, and sawmills.

Houston is now the fastest-growing city in the country. It is the home of NASA's Johnson Space Center, which controlled the U.S. moon flights, and it is the headquarters for many oil companies. Its famous medical center is a leader in treatment of heart disease and cancer. The city contains skyscrapers, several universities, and the Astrodome.

What was once Buffalo Bayou is now the Houston Ship Channel. Factories and refineries line its banks, and ships of all nations steam up and down its waters.

The Port of Houston is one of the busiest in the world. Each year about 4,500 ships from sixty lands load and unload their cargoes at its wharves. That foreign trade is worth ten billion dollars each year— more than is handled at any other U.S. port except New York City.

The Allen brothers' dream for their little town on the bayou has more than come true.

Opposite:
Houston's towering skyline and interlacing freeways are reflected in the water of Buffalo Bayou.

The stately "Shadows on the Teche" still stands beneath towering trees in New Iberia, Louisiana. Built in the 1830s, it is now a museum.

8

Wealth from the Bayou

THE BAYOUS PLAYED an important role in the early history of the South, and they are just as important today. The harvest of food from the water is enormous, and it becomes more important as our demand for food increases.

Coastal estuaries—shallow bays and streams that contain a mixture of fresh and salt water—are the most productive areas on earth. These brackish waters are kept at the proper salt content as fresh water comes down the rivers and bayous and mixes with salt water from the sea. According to the U.S. Fish and Wildlife Service, nearly ninety percent of all the fish and shellfish harvested on the Texas coast depend on these estuaries for survival. Most are hatched and grow in the shallow waters. An acre of estuary can produce ten times as much protein as an acre of America's richest farmland.

A crab fisherman loads his catch of blue crabs into boxes for shipment to restaurants.

Louisiana is famous for its crayfish, or crawfish. Up to ten million pounds are caught each year in the Atchafalaya Basin alone. Crawfish farms are made by flooding fields with water from the bayous.

When most people think of fur trapping, they think of the cold north country. In fact, it surprises most people to learn that Louisiana is the leading fur-producing area in North America. In some years, the state produces more pelts than all of Canada and Alaska combined. As many as sixty-five percent of all U.S. furs come from Louisiana.

In pioneer times, furs were obtained by trading with the northern Indians. Then white trappers began to catch their own. Getting the furs out of the northern wilderness presented a problem, however.

Fur traders found no such problem in Louisiana. The bayous were like open roads, and the furs could be brought out by boat. Other fur-laden boats came down the Mississippi River. New Orleans quickly became a major fur-trading center.

The swamps and marshes of the bayou country shelter muskrats, mink, raccoons, otters, opossums, and skunks. All are valuable for their furs. After nutria escaped into the Louisiana marshes, they became the most important fur-bearing animals of all.

From the trees in the forests and swamps of the bayou country, we get lumber that is used for making thousands of things—from houses, paper, and bridges to toothpicks, chemicals, and baseball bats.

In more recent years, the bayou is becoming a center for the production of oil and natural gas. Some of the oil wells that now dot the landscape have been

These wells in the bayou have been producing oil and natural gas for many years.

Opposite:
The raccoon is one of the major fur-bearing mammals of the bayou country.

producing energy for many years; others have been drilled only recently. The search for more oil is still going on.

Beneath the earth are great beds of salt, formed millions of years ago in ancient seas. Because salt is lighter than the surrounding rock, it is squeezed upward into the layers above by the pressures within the earth. These great pillars of salt may be hundreds of feet thick and are called salt domes. Oil and gas are trapped along the sides of these formations. Sometimes, if they are near the surface, the salt domes push up the ground into low, rounded hills that rise above the surrounding countryside.

Avery Island is such a salt dome. It is an island of high ground in the middle of a marsh, rather than an island in open water. There are several such islands along the Texas and Louisiana coasts. Most have oil wells, and some also have salt mines. Old plantation homes and even small towns have been built on these hills.

The discovery of oil brought new people and a new way of life to the bayous. Instead of farming or hunting and fishing, many of the residents now work in the oil fields. The waterways bustle with boats, loaded with pipe and equipment. Helicopters roar overhead on the way to platforms in the Gulf of Mexico. Getting energy from the ground is now the biggest business along the bayou.

Bayous are also places in which to play. They provide recreation for young and old alike. People hunt and fish, canoe, and camp along the bayous, and some of the land in the bayou country has been set

Bayous provide recreation for many people.

aside as parks. The Big Thicket National Preserve in Texas has several beautiful bayous flowing through its forests and swamps. They provide water for rare plants and for the hundreds of animals that live on the banks.

In a city, a bayou is an oasis of green in a concrete desert. It may have trails for running, walking, or biking. These things are important, too.

Progress, however, has also brought problems to the bayous. As more people come there to live, there is less room for wildlife. Trees hewn for lumber no longer shade wild flowers or provide acorns for squirrels. Dams stop some streams from flowing and make lakes out of others. Automobiles and factories pollute the air. The oil and chemicals that are so important to our way of life often get into the waters and kill wildlife.

While becoming one of the greatest seaports in the world, the Houston Ship Channel also became one of its most polluted waterways. The city poured its sewage into the channel, and the industries along the banks did the same thing with their wastes. Cans and bottles floated in patches of oil. Soon no fish remained.

There are stories about criminals who jumped into the channel when chased by police—only to climb right out again with burning eyes and skin. The water became so foul that it ate away the propellers of the ships docked at the wharves.

New laws and controls on pollution, and a greater concern for improving the environment, have cleaned up the Houston Ship Channel a little. The water looks cleaner and smells better, and a few fish are returning. But it is not, by any means, the pretty Buffalo Bayou it was when the Indians camped on its banks.

Egrets hunt for food in the shadow of a huge power plant.

Fortunately, this is the worst example of pollution in the bayous; few others are as bad. Most are still homes for fish and water lilies.

Even harder to control and evaluate is the effect of changing the entire face of the land, of clearing forests and building subdivisions, of draining swamps and digging canals.

The population of the entire country is increasing, and that of the South is growing even faster. This means more houses, more shopping centers, and more paper mills and chemical plants. Small towns have become cities that sprawl in all directions. All of this takes space, which means cutting down trees and plowing up prairies. This destroys native plants and habitats for animals. But there are more long-range effects, too. When the trees and grass are gone, there is nothing to stop the rain from running off the land. Then there are floods and erosion.

To stop the flooding, new drainage ditches are dug and dams are built. Natural bayous are "channelized," or straightened and lined with concrete, to help them carry more water. Then there is even less habitat for wildlife. The bayou becomes nothing but a ditch. It is indeed a vicious circle.

The important coastal marshes are being filled in to create new land for waterfront homes or industrial plants. But these are the same estuaries that are needed for producing fish, shrimp, and crabs. They are required to feed our growing population.

What is the answer? There is no easy solution. Somewhere, somehow, we must find room for both people and nature along the bayous.

9

Hope for the Future

THE TOTAL PICTURE, of course, is not all dark. In spite
of the tremendous human pressure and use of the land,
many bayous remain wild and pure. There are still bogs
full of orchids and carnivorous plants, and there are
still bobcats, bullfrogs, barred owls, and alligators.
Due to laws controlling the use of DDT and other
insecticides, the ospreys, brown pelicans, and bald
eagles seem to be increasing in number again. Hope-
fully, the population of Louisiana's state bird, the
pelican, will rapidly increase. Catches of fur-bearing
animals in the Louisiana bayous have not decreased in
the last two decades, and the number of crabs caught
on the Texas coast is at an all-time high.

All of these are signs that at least part of the bayou
country is surviving the pressure of the present. What
the future holds will depend on how we continue to
manage this vital natural treasure. Many national

groups are concerned with the preservation of the bayous. The National Audubon Society, National Wildlife Federation, and Sierra Club are dedicated to saving the wild areas. Other state and local groups are working to preserve particular bayous. For example, groups in Louisiana are attempting to save the Atchafalaya from channelization which would kill the great swamp.

Some battles to preserve the environment will be won; others will be lost. Yet the effort is an important one, and it depends on everyone, wherever he or she might live.

10

A Happy Ending

NOT MORE THAN twenty miles from downtown Houston is a stretch of brackish water called Armand Bayou. It flows past freeways, shopping centers, chemical plants, and the National Aeronautics and Space Administration's Johnson Space Center.

Here, in the shadow of the moon flights' Mission Control lies a wild bayou—a peaceful refuge for birds and animals. It is a place where people can walk in a field of wild flowers or sit quietly on a moss-covered log beneath towering oaks. The bayou was first called Middle Bayou when pioneers settled on its banks to farm. But it was renamed Armand Bayou in honor of Armand Yramategui, a former curator of the Houston Museum of Natural Science's Burke Baker Planetarium.

Armand loved the bayou, and he considered it the best preserved natural area in the country. At the time

A sight-seeing boat on Armand Bayou.

Opposite:
Nature center director Rick Pratt works with
an injured hawk that will soon be well enough
to release.

of his death in 1970, he had been urging the community to set it aside as a nature center and refuge.

Friends, civic groups, companies, and local governments all joined the fight to save Armand's bayou. They were able to set aside more than 2,000 acres of forests, fields, and tidal swamps. Now the area contains a large building with laboratories, a library, and a classroom. Many visitors follow trails through the woods, accompanied by trained naturalists who explain the secrets of the bayou. There are classes in pioneer skills. The nature center staff treats and releases birds and mammals that are injured or orphaned, and scientists from nearby universities do research on the ecology.

Armand Bayou is not only a refuge for the plants and animals that live there. It is also a refuge in which people can spend a quiet moment in the wilderness and forget the busy world of the city. It is everything a bayou should be. And it is hoped that Armand Bayou Nature Center is a good beginning that will grow and spread to other bayous.

Index

Acadia, 58
Acadian, 58, 60, 61
Acadian Village, *59*
Alabama, 5
Alaska, 71
Allen brothers, 64, 65, 67
Alligator, 1, *2,* 3, 38, *39,* 40, 62, 79
Amphibians, 43
Anglos, 60
Anhinga, 35, *37*
Anole, green, 42, *52*
Archaeology, 63
Arkansas, 5
Armadillo, 29, *32,* 33
Armand Bayou, 81, *82-83,* 84
Atchafalaya, 61, 62, 71, 80
Attakapa, 58
Avery Island, 54, 55, 74

Barataria Bay, 64
Bass, largemouth, 24, 62
Bats, 3, 26
Bayou, definition, 5, *6-7,* 8
Bayou City, 63
Bayuk, 5

Bear, black, 53
Beaver, 3, 24, 26
Beetles, 47
Big Thicket, 63, 76
Birds, 11, 33, 40, 49, 53, 81, 84
    migration, 33
Blackbirds, 35
Bladderwort, *21,* 22
Bluebirds, 38, 56
Bobcat, 3, 29, 79
Bog, 20, 79
Bouef, 58
Bream, 24, 62
Bromeliad, 17, *18-19,* 20
Buffalo Bayou, 64, 65, *66,* 67, 76
Bunting: indigo, 33
    painted, 33
Burke Baker Planetarium, 81
Butterflies, 3, 47
    gulf fritillary, *45*
    swallowtail, 47
Butterwort, *21,* 22

Cajun, 58
Canada, 33, 58, 60, 71
Cardinal, 35

85

Carnivorous plants, 20, *21,* 22, 79
Caterpillars, 51, *52*
Catfish, 24, 62
Central America, 33
Chameleon, 42
Channelization, 78, 80
Chat, yellow-breasted, *34*
Chêne, 17
Chenier, 17, 33
Chickadee, 38
Chitimacha, 58
Chlorophyll, 20
Choctaw, 5, 61
Civil War, 61
Clams, 3, 24
   corbicula (Asian), 56, 63
Coot, *15*
Cotton, 60
Cougar (panther), 53
Coyote, 29
Coypu, 55
Crabs, 24, 51, 62, *70,* 78, 79
Crane, whooping, 53
Crappie, 24, 62
Crayfish, 24, *25,* 26, 62, 71
Creeks, 8
Croaker, 24

DDT, 53, 79
Deer, white-tailed, 29, *30,* 62
Delta, 57
Dragonflies, *46,* 47, 51
Drum, 24
Ducks, 35, 49, 62
   wood, 38

Eagle, bald, 53, 62, 79
Ecology, 51, 84
Egrets, 54, *77*
   great, *36*
Endangered species, 40, 53
Estuaries, 69
Europe, 55, 60
Evangeline, 60

Ferns, 20
Fish, 23-24, 40, 51, 53, 69, 76, 78

   as food, 26, *27,* 35, 43
Fishing, 24, 61, 62, 63, 74
Flies, 43
Flounder, 24
Flowers, wild, 11, 14, 51, 53, 76,
   81
Food chain, 51, *52*
Fox: gray, 29
   red, 29
French, 5, 58, 60, 64
Frogs, 3, 26, 42, 43
   bullfrog, 43, *44,* 62, 79
   chorus, 43
   cricket, 43
   green treefrog, *12*
   treefrog, 11, 43
Fur trade, 24, 55, 71, 79

Galveston Bay, 65
Gar, alligator, 23
Gaspergou, 24
Geese, 35, 49, 62
Grass, 14, *15,* 24, 51
Grosbeak: blue, 33
   rose-breasted, 33
Gulf Coast, 14, 26, 38
Gulf of Mexico, 14, 17, 24, 33,
   51, 63, 74
Gulls, 35

Hawks, 51, *83*
   red-shouldered, 35
Herons, 35
   great blue, 1
Houston, 63-65, *66,* 67, 81
   Museum of Natural Science, 81
   Port of, 67
   Ship Channel, 67, 76
Houston, Sam, 64
Hunting, 53, 61, 62, 63, 74
Hurricane, 17, 55

Indians, 58, 60, 64, 71, 76
Insecticide, 53, 79
Insects, 11, 43, 47
   as food, 3, 20, 22, 26, 33, 38,
   42, 43

Introduced species, 54-56
Jay, blue, 35
Johnson Space Center, 65, 81

Lafitte, Jean, 64
Lafourche, 58
Lizard, 42, 43, 51
  glass, 42-43
Longfellow, Henry W., 60
Louisiana, 5, 14, 29, 33, 53, 54,
  55, 57-62, 64, 71, 74, 79, 80
Lumber, 71, 76

Mammals, 11, 40, 51, 84
Marsh, 14, 17
  brackish, 17, 69
  fresh, 14
  salt, 14
Marsupial, 29
McIlhenny, Edward, 54
Mexico, 8, 33, 64
Mice, 26, 40
Midden heap, 64
Middle Bayou, 81
Mink, 26, 71
Minnows, 23-24
Mississippi, 5
Mississippi River, 57, 60, 61, 64,
  71
Mockingbird, 35
Mole, 26
Mosquitoes, 43, 47, 64
Mullet, 24
Muskrat, 26, 71

NASA, 65, 81
National Audubon Society, 80
National Wildlife Federation, 80
Native Americans, 58, 60, 63
Natural gas, 71, *73*
New Orleans, 54, 58, 71
New York, 55, 64, 67
Nova Scotia, 58
Nutria, 26, 55, 71

Oak motte, 17, 33
Oil, 61, 63, 65, 71, *73*, 74, 76

Opossum, 29, *31*, 62, 71
Orchids, 20, 79
Orioles, 33
Osprey, 53, 79
Otter, 3, 26, *27*, 71
Owl: barred, 3, 35, 79
  great horned, 3, *50*
  screech, 3, 38
Oyster, 63

Pelican, brown, 53, 79
Perch, 24
Pigeon, passenger, 53
Pirate, 64
Pirogue, 62
Pitcher-plant, 20, *21*
Plant associations, 9
Plant communities, 9
Plantation, 60, 74
Plaquemine, 58
Poaching, 40
Pocket gopher, 26
Pollution, 76, 78
Pratt, Rick, *83*

Rabbit: cottontail, 29
  swamp, 29
Raccoon, 3, 29, 56, 62, 71, *72*
Rats, 26, 40
Recreation, 74, *75*, 76
Redfish, 24
Reptiles, 38
Republic of Texas, 64, 65
Rice, 26, 55
Rio Grande, 33
Rivers, 8
Rodents, 26, 35, 55
Roosevelt, Theodore, 53

St. Martinville, 60
Salamander, 43
Salt dome, 17, 74
Sandpipers, 35
Shakespeare, William, 55
Shellfish, 51, 69
Shorebirds, 49
Shrews, 26

87

Shrimp, 24, 51, 78
Shrubs, 11, 53
Sierra Club, 80
Skunk, 29, 71
Snails, 24
Snakes, 40, 42, 51, 60
  broad-banded water, *41*
  canebrake rattlesnake, 40
  copperhead, 40
  coral, 40
  cottonmouth, 40, *41*, 62
  earth, 42
  garter, 42
  green, 42
  hognose, 42
  king, 42
  poisonous, 40-41
  pygmy rattlesnake, 40
  racer, 42
  rat, 42
  ribbon, 42
  water, 42
  water moccasin, 40
South America, 26, 33, 54, 55
Spanish, 58, 64
Spanish moss, 3, 17, *18-19*, 20,
  53-54, 62
Sphagnum moss, 20
Spiders, 51, 60-61
Squirrels, 62, 76
  flying, 3, 26, *28*
  fox, 26
  gray, 26
Starling, 55
Sugarcane, 26, 55, 60
Sundew, *21*, 22
Sunfish, 24
Swamp, 11, 14, 17, 20, 61

Tanager, scarlet, 33, *34*
Taylor, Richard, 61
Teche, 58, 60, 61
Terns, 35
Texas, 5, 33, 63-67, 69, 74, 76, 79
Thrushes, 33
  wood, 35
Tides, 14
Titmouse, 38

Toads, 43
Trees, 11, 53
  beech, 9
  button-bush, 35
  cypress, 11, *13*, 14, 35, 58, 62
  deciduous, 9
  dogwood, 9
  elm, 9
  evergreen, 9, 11, 14, 17
  hackberry, 9
  hardwood, 9, 11
  holly, 9
  ironwood, 9
  live oak, 17, 22, 33, 60
  maple, 9
  oak, 9, 81
  pine, 11, 14
  redbud, 9
  southern magnolia, 9, *10*
  tupelo, 11
  willow, 35
Trembling prairie, 14
Turtle, 1, 40, 62
  alligator snapping, 43
  box, 43
  common snapping, 43
  map, 43
  mud, 43
  painted, 43
  slider, 43
  soft-shelled, 43

Vines, 11
Vireos, 33

Warblers, 33
  prothonotary, 38
Water hyacinth, 14, 54-55
Water lily, 14, *16*, 78
Weather, 35, 49
Wolf, red, 53
Woodpeckers, 38
  ivory-billed, 53
  pileated, 38
Wren, Carolina, 35

Yramategui, Armand, 81